# Contents

# Introduction

# India today – the land and people

*India is one of the most densely populated countries in the world. Today, one-seventh of the world's population lives in India alone. China is the only country in the world with more people than India. India's population is growing at a rate of about 15 million a year.*

*What are the land and people like in this vast and populous country?*

## A world of contrasts

India is in the area of the world known today as South Asia. South Asia includes India, Pakistan, Bangladesh, Sri Lanka, Nepal, Bhutan and the Maldives. The area covers over four million square kilometres and includes great rivers like the Ganges, and great mountain ranges like the Himalayas, as well as deserts, deltas and fertile plains.

The peoples of South Asia are very varied. In India alone there are 14 official languages, and over 1,500 other languages. Several of the major religions of the world are practised in South Asia: most people in India are Hindus, but the majority of the people in Pakistan and Bangladesh are Muslims.

For 5,000 years India has been one of the main centres of civilisation in the world. Some of the first cities in the world were built 4,500 years ago along the Indus Valley.

In the sixteenth century most of India was conquered by a family of princes called the Mughals. They came from lands that are now part of Afghanistan and Uzbekistan. This book is about the rise and fall of their brilliant empire, and the British Raj (rule) which replaced it.

*India's position in the world*

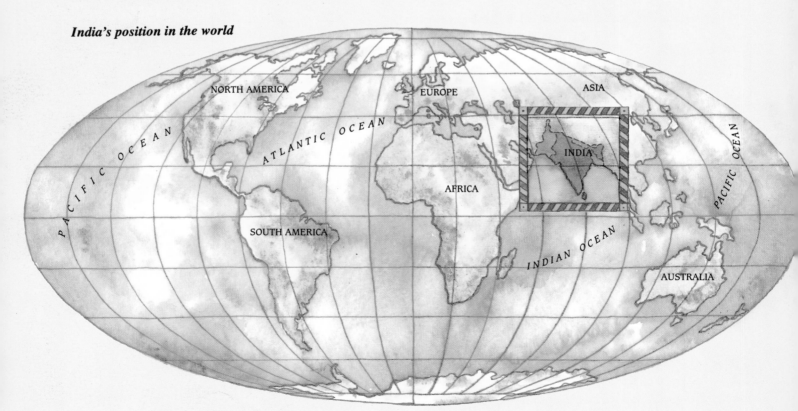

# India

## From Mughal Empire to British Raj

Paul Goalen
Head of History
Homerton College, Cambridge

CAMBRIDGE
UNIVERSITY PRESS

Published by the Press Syndicate of the University of Cambridge
The Pitt Building, Trumpington Street, Cambridge CB2 1RP
40 West 20th Street, New York, NY 10011–4211, USA
10 Stamford Road, Oakleigh, Victoria 3166, Australia

© Cambridge University Press 1992

First published 1992

Printed in Hong Kong by Wing King Tong Co., Ltd.

A catalogue record for this book is available from the British
Library.

ISBN 0 521 40781 8

*Cover illustration:* An Indian ruler in procession, about 1770.
The Maratha chief, Tuljaji, is shown surrounded by his retainers.
Victoria and Albert Museum.

Designed and produced by Gecko Limited, Bicester, Oxon

## Notice to teachers

Many of the sources used in this textbook have been
adapted or abridged from the original.

## Acknowledgements

18 Birmingham City Museum and Art Gallery; 39 (left),
41, 43 from *Echoes of Old Calcutta* by H. E. Busteed,
Irish University Press, 1882 (Bodleian Library); 56 (top),
58 from *History of the Indian Mutiny* by Charles Ball,
London Printing and Publishing Company, 1858
(Bodleian Library); 13, 17, 18, 20, 21, 29, 30, 32, 34, 38,
48, 52, 55, 59 British Library/India Office Library and
Records; 49 British Library/IOLR (Bridgeman Art
Library, London); 16, 27 (bottom) Cambridge University
Press; 5 (top left, top right, bottom right), 28, 32–33, 38
Robert Harding Picture Library; 31 (right) His Highness
the Maharaga of Satara (Robert Harding Picture Library);
60 (bottom) Hulton Picture Company; 15 Keir Collection,
England (photo A. A Barnes); 10 Khuda Bakhsh Oriental
Public Library, Patna (Robert Harding Picture Library); 46
National Army Museum; 40 National Portrait Gallery; 39
(right) Powis Castle, National Trust Picture Library;
60–61 (background) Panos Pictures; 60 (top) Popperfoto
Ltd.; 51 Prince of Wales Museum of Western India,
Bombay; 57, 58 Punch Publications Ltd.; 9 Raza Library,
Rampur (Robert Harding Picture Library); 45 The Board
of Trustees of the Royal Armouries; 31 (left) School of
Oriental and African Studies; 56 (bottom) from *Complete
Narrative of the Mutiny in India . . .* by Thomas Frost
(ed.), London, Reed, 1858 (University Library,
Cambridge); 11, 12, 14, 23, 27 (top), 45 (left), 46–47, 50
Victoria and Albert Museum; 5 (bottom left) Zefa Ltd.

858 million

121 million    119 million

INDIA    BANGLADESH    PAKISTAN

*The population of South Asia.*

Christians 2.5%    Sikhs 2.0%    Others 1.5%

Muslims
11%

Hindus
83%

*The peoples of South Asia.*

*The hot, dusty desert of Rajasthan.*

*The Himalayas are the greatest mountains in the world. Ama Khablam is close to Mount Everest, the highest mountain of all.*

AFGHANISTAN

CHINA

PAKISTAN

Chenab

Sutlej

Indus

Himalayas

Mt Everest
8,848m

NEPAL    ②    BHUTAN

Brahmaputra

Thar Desert

Jumna    ④

Ganges

BANGLADESH

①

INDIA

Narmada

Deccan
Plateau

BURMA

Godavari

ARABIAN
SEA

Western Ghats

Eastern Ghats

Krishna

BAY OF BENGAL

Andaman Is.

Laccadive Is.

③

Nicobar Is.

SRI LANKA

Maldives

INDIAN OCEAN

0    500km

③ *Tea plantation in the Nilgiri Hills.*

④ *The river Ganges at Varanasi.*

*The land of India and the variety of its landscapes.*

*During the sixteenth and seventeenth centuries, the Mughals conquered almost all of South Asia. They were a powerful Muslim family who came from lands that are now part of Afghanistan and Uzbekistan. The Mughal emperors ruled over a largely Hindu population for nearly 200 years.*

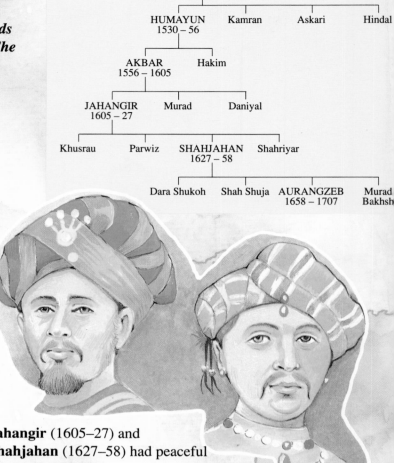

```
                        BABUR
                       1526 – 30

        HUMAYUN          Kamran      Askari      Hindal
        1530 – 56

    AKBAR        Hakim
    1556 – 1605

JAHANGIR     Murad      Daniyal
1605 – 27

Khusrau   Parwiz   SHAHJAHAN   Shahriyar
                   1627 – 58

              Dara Shukoh   Shah Shuja   AURANGZEB    Murad
                                         1658 – 1707  Bakhsh
```

**Babur** (1526–30) was the first Mughal emperor. He conquered much of northern India between 1526 and 1530. In 1526 he defeated the ruler of Delhi, Ibrahim Lodi, at the first battle of Panipat.

**Jahangir** (1605–27) and **Shahjahan** (1627–58) had peaceful reigns. This helped the economy to grow and made it possible for the Mughal emperors to spend huge amounts of money on beautiful paintings and magnificent buildings.

**Akbar** (1556–1605) was perhaps the most successful of the Mughal emperors. He ruled India at the same time as Queen Elizabeth I ruled England. His empire was vast – about as large as the whole of Europe put together. He was both a brave soldier and a good organiser. He rewarded loyal nobles with lands. Although he was a Muslim, he allowed people to follow the religion of their choice.

**Aurangzeb** (1658–1707) was the last of the great Mughals. During his reign the Mughal Empire expanded deep into southern India. However Aurangzeb annoyed many people by his hostility to the Hindu religion, and he had to fight many wars to keep the empire together.

# Mughal Empire

Extent of Mughal Empire 1530
Extent of Mughal Empire 1605
Extent of Mughal Empire 1707

Kabul

KASHMIR

*Indus*

KANGRA

*Chenab*

Lahore

*Himalayas*

PUNJAB

*Sutlej*

*Brahmaputra*

BALUCHISTAN

*Indus*

HARYANA

KUMAUN

*Panipat*

RAJPUTANA

Delhi

DOAB

AWADH

SIND

Agra

ASSAM

RAJASTHAN

Fatehpur Sikri

*Jumna*

Benares

*Ganges*

BENGAL

BIHAR

Patna

CUTCH

Ahmadabad

GONDWANA

Dacca

KATHIAWAR

GUJARAT

*Narmada*

Surat

KHANDESH

ORISSA

BERAR

ARAKANESE

*ARABIAN SEA*

NIZAMSHAHIS

*Godavari*

*BAY OF BENGAL*

ADILSHAHIS

DECCAN

Bijapur

Golconda

QUTBSHAHIS

*Krishna*

MARATHAS

Goa

0    500
km

# 1
# Babur the victorious

*Babur conquered much of north India between 1526 and 1530. His victory in 1526 over Ibrahim Lodi,
the ruler of Delhi, was the first step towards setting up the Mughal Empire.*

**How did Babur defeat the powerful ruler, Ibrahim Lodi?**

### An invitation to India

Babur, the first Mughal emperor, was born far from India, in modern Uzbekistan. His early life was exciting and dangerous. After many adventures he made himself ruler of the city of Kabul, in Afghanistan.

Before the Mughals, India was made up of many small states ruled by kings. The ruler of Delhi, Ibrahim Lodi, was one of the most important of these kings. In 1525, one of Ibrahim's enemies invited Babur to overthrow Ibrahim. The two sides came face to face in 1526 at the battle of Panipat.

### Firepower

Babur had new light field guns and muskets, and combined them with more traditional cavalry (horsemen) and archers. The effect was devastating.

### Babur is outnumbered

Babur's army consisted of about 12,000 men, including skilled cavalry and expert musketmen and artillerymen. He faced Ibrahim's army of 100,000 men and 1,000 elephants.

Before the battle, Babur placed his light field artillery behind small ramparts and tied the guns together with leather thongs so that Ibrahim's cavalry could not easily storm them. When Ibrahim's army came to a halt in front of these defences, Babur sent his archers on horseback to the back of the enemy so that Ibrahim's men were caught between gunfire and showers of arrows. Ibrahim Lodi and most of his men died on the battlefield.

## Source A
**Babur dictating his memoirs to a secretary in a garden.** *From a 17th-century manuscript. Beautiful gardens were very important to the new Mughal rulers. They provided welcome shade from the summer sun. They were also a reminder of life and pleasure in Kabul. The Mughal rulers were buried in tomb gardens. Babur was buried in his favourite garden in Kabul.*

- *In this picture Babur's memoirs are being written down by a scribe. Do you think this affects their reliability?*

## Source B
Babur describes the battle in his memoirs.

'God made this victory easy for us! The battle was over in half a day; 5–6,000 men were killed close to Ibrahim. We counted at least another 15 or 16,000 dead elsewhere on the battlefield; other [Hindu] estimates put the total dead at around 40–50,000.

Those who fled the battlefield were pursued; our men captured nobles of every rank. During the afternoon, Ibrahim's body was found in a heap of the dead; his head was brought to my court.'

Babur, *Baburnama*, 1526–30

### After Panipat
Babur died in 1530, four years after the defeat of Ibrahim. He fought more important battles and each time, with the help of his guns, he was victorious. By the time of his death, Babur controlled northern India, and the Mughal Empire had been founded.

1 Explain in your own words why Babur fought Ibrahim Lodi.

2 How many reasons can you find to explain why Babur won the battle of Panipat? Which do you think was the most important reason?

3 Source B was written by Babur's scribe. There are no written sources from people who fought on the other side. Why do you think this causes problems for historians?

# 2

# Akbar: the making of a Mughal emperor

*After Babur's death in 1530, his son Humayun became emperor. Humayun ruled until he died in a fall down his library stairs in 1556. His son Akbar became the new Mughal emperor, aged only 13.*

*What sort of a person was the young Akbar?*

**The war against Hemu**

Akbar had to be a very strong ruler to keep and extend his empire. A Hindu general called Hemu tried to stop Akbar from becoming emperor. Each side had an army and they fought each other at the second battle of Panipat in November 1556.

## Source A

Here is how Abul Fazl, who wrote the story of Akbar's life – his biography – describes the lucky accident that led to a Mughal victory.

'Hemu rode on top of Hawai, his best elephant. He fought very bravely, but in the middle of the battle Hemu was hit in the eye by an arrow which pierced the socket and came out at the back of his head … When his soldiers saw this, they lost heart and fled.'

Abul Fazl, *Akbarnama*, about 1590

## Source B  *A victory tower made out of the enemies' heads.*
*Painted in about 1590. This was a custom of the earlier Mughal emperors.*
● *What effect do you think a tower like this would have on people?*

Hemu's body was brought before Akbar and was beheaded. His head was sent to Kabul and his body was sent to Delhi to be placed on a gibbet as a warning to others. Those who had supported Hemu were killed and their heads were made into a victory tower.

## Source C

Here is a modern historian's account of Akbar's early life.

'He had had an unsettled childhood, shuttled like a pawn between his father and his uncles, and from a very early age he had taken an active part in military affairs. At 10, he was beside his father in battle, and was given the leadership of his dead uncle Hindal's followers. At 12 he was with the advance guard, and nominally in command of it, during the victory at Sirhind. As a boy in Kabul he had terrified everyone by his passion for riding fierce camels.'

Bamber Gascoigne, *The Great Moghuls*, 1971

● What was Akbar like as a boy?

### Young Akbar takes charge

Akbar never learnt to read or write but he had a sharp mind and superb memory which helped him become a strong leader.

At first Akbar had little real power because his empire was run by a rich and powerful minister called Bairam Khan. In 1560, when he was 18, Akbar took over control of the government by ordering Khan to go on a pilgrimage to the holy city of Makkah (in Arabia). Bairam Khan was killed on this dangerous journey.

Another threat to young Akbar's power was his cruel and ambitious foster-brother Adham Khan. In 1562 Akbar had Adham Khan thrown to his death from the palace walls as punishment for murdering one of Akbar's ministers.

● Why do you think Akbar never learnt to read or write?

Source D  *Akbar has Adham Khan thrown to his death from the parapet of his palace. Akbar was just 19, and now fully in charge of the Mughal Empire. This picture was painted in about 1590.*

1 Explain in your own words how Hemu died.

2 What can we learn from Source C about Akbar's character?

3 Young Akbar destroyed Hemu, dismissed Bairam Khan and killed Adham Khan. Do you think this shows that he was a bad man?

11

# 3

# Akbar's empire

*By 1576, Akbar controlled an empire of 100 million people. He remained firmly in control of this enormous state until his death in 1605.*

*Why was Akbar so successful?*

## The court: a city on the move

The heart of the empire was Akbar's court. This included his family, servants, ministers and nobles. Akbar's court did not have a permanent home in one of the great Mughal cities like Delhi, Agra or Lahore. It was always on the move, conquering or reconquering, hunting or putting down rebellions.

When the court and the army were on the march together, it was like a moving city of some 200,000 to 300,000 people, with vast quantities of tents, baggage and furniture carried by some 50,000 horses and oxen. The emperor's tents were usually sent in advance. They were so large that it could take a week for 1,000 men to put them up. Akbar introduced the idea of a large cart containing several bathrooms which was pulled by an elephant.

Inside the tent-city would be found all the usual buildings of a royal palace: a mosque, and the harem (women's quarters) of 5,000 women, including Akbar's 300 wives.

## Choosing good courtiers

Such a court needed vast amounts of money. It was the centre of attention for ambitious men and women. Akbar used these people to help him control his huge empire. He was careful in choosing people for important jobs: often he ordered portraits of officers to be painted, to help him assess their characters before they came to court.

## Source B

Abul Fazl, Akbar's friend and chronicler, explains the importance of portrait painting.

'His majesty himself sat for his portrait, and also ordered pictures of all the nobles of the realm. An immense album was thus formed: those that have passed away have received a new life, and those who are still alive have immortality promised them.'

Abul Fazl, *Ain-i-Akbari*, about 1590

*Khwagagi Muhammad, 1598.*

*Zain Khan Kokah, 1595.*

## Source C  *Two Mughal noblemen.*

## The mansabdars: loyal supporters of Akbar

The officers of his army were very important for Akbar's government. There were thirty-three *mansabs* (ranks or grades): the lowest was a commander of 10 cavalrymen, and the highest had 5,000 cavalrymen at his command.

The lower-ranking *mansabdars* (rank-holding officers) were paid in cash, but a noble with a rank of 500 cavalrymen or more would usually be given a *jagir*. This was a large piece of land with poor farmers living on it: they paid taxes to the noble. This gave the noble a salary and paid for his cavalry.

A mansabdar would usually be given a new job every three or four years and new lands as part of his promotion. This stopped mansabdars from staying too long in one place where they might build up a lot of personal support locally, which could be used in rebellion against the emperor.

## The army: keeping the empire in order

The mansab system provided Akbar with a large army of well-equipped cavalry provided at the mansabdars' expense. The mansabdar knew that he would not gain further promotion if he failed in this duty, or forgot to give expensive presents to the emperor.

The military power of the Mughals depended on the cavalry provided by the mansabdars. There were 100 million people in Akbar's realm and many were possible rebels. Peace was maintained by well-armed cavalrymen stationed in towns and along the important trade routes. The mansabdar would also be expected to provide cavalry to put down any major rebellions.

## Akbar the hunter

When Akbar heard that there was about to be trouble, he would move a hunting expedition towards an area of unrest. He would use hundreds of soldiers as beaters to drive the game towards the hunting party. Such a display of power usually frightened people so that they did not rebel.

Source D *Akbar hunting with cheetahs. Akbar loved hunting with specially trained cheetahs. They had collars studded with jewels and were taken on the hunt sitting blindfolded on beautiful carpets. Bets would be placed on which cheetah would kill most deer during the day.*

● *How does the hunting in this picture compare with hunting today?*

## Religious tolerance: a fair deal for Hindus

One of Akbar's most important policies which helped him to control India was that of religious tolerance. The Mughal conquerors of India were Muslims, but most of their people were Hindus with different customs and beliefs. Akbar was determined to prevent religious differences from causing trouble.

In order to show his Hindu subjects that he trusted them, Akbar made several important changes. First he married a Hindu princess from Rajputana in 1562. (She became the mother of the next emperor, Jahangir.) This was a wise move because the Rajputs were famous as some of the greatest warriors in India. They now served the Mughals loyally for the next 100 years.

Leading Hindus were also given high ranks in the Mughal civil service, and in 1563 Akbar abolished the tax on pilgrimages to Hindu shrines. In 1564 he got rid of the hated *jizya*, a poll tax which previous Muslim rulers had forced Hindus to pay. Hindus were now allowed to build temples freely and to celebrate public festivals. Prisoners of war were no longer forced to become Muslims. Akbar even grew his hair long like a Hindu, and occasionally wore the *tilak*, the Hindu ornamental mark on the forehead.

Source E *Brahmin and Muslim learned man in dispute. Mughal School, early 17th century. Akbar encouraged religious debate.*

---

**1** Look at Source A. What signs of wealth and success can you see?

**2** What support (not shown in Source A) would Akbar have needed to conquer Surat?

**3** Study Sources B and C. How do they help you understand Akbar's success? If you had been Akbar, to which of the noblemen in Source C would you have given an important job? Give your reasons.

**4** Source D shows Akbar hunting with cheetahs. Make a list of the possible reasons why Akbar might wish to go hunting.

**5** Make a list of the reasons why you think Akbar was so successful. Divide your list into the more important reasons and less important reasons, and set them in a table.

15

# 4

# Village life

*Whilst the Mughals ruled India in luxury, most of their subjects lived in villages, and many of them were very poor.*

*What was life like for the poor people in India?*

## People in an Indian village.

### The zamindar
He was the most important landholder in the village. Sometimes he was responsible for collecting the taxes for the Mughal emperor.

### Poor peasants
These might include peasants who came from other villages; peasants who rented land from rich peasants or the zamindar; or very poor peasants who had no land but helped with the harvest.

### Rich peasants
They often had documents to prove their claim to the land they farmed. They usually claimed to be descended from the first farmers in the village.

Source A   *Figures of caste-'types', late 19th century.*

## Village homes and palaces

Poor peasant families often lived in single-roomed mud huts with thatched roofs. These contrasted starkly with the Mughal palaces.

Inside a poor peasant's hut there would be hardly any furniture except perhaps for bamboo or straw mats. Many peasants had no shoes to wear. Cloth was expensive, so their clothes were made of very coarse material.

## Giant dams and fish manure

Although many Indians were poor, farming methods were not primitive. The ploughs used were similar to those used in England during the seventeenth century. Indians living near the coast used fish manure as fertiliser. Machinery was used when sowing seed, and crops were changed from year to year to get the best yield from the land. Irrigation was also common: wells and tanks were dug, and a variety of methods used to lift the water into field channels.

Sometimes huge dams were built to make vast lakes for irrigation, like Dhebar Lake in Mewar which was 58 kilometres (36 miles) in circumference. Canals for irrigation were also cut, particularly in north India. For example, Shahjahan's canal – Nahr-i-Faiz – was 240 kilometres (150 miles) long.

**Source B** *A typical village scene in India. Drawn by George Chinnery in 1813.*

## A simple diet

The poorest peasants ate only once a day. On the western coast of India this meal might consist of a mixture of boiled rice, millet and grass roots. Even in wheat-growing areas like Agra and Delhi, the poor would sell their wheat and eat cheaper, coarser grains themselves. Fish was rare except near the coast and rivers, and there was a religious ban on eating pork and beef.

Many peasants could not afford expensive spices like cloves, cardamoms or pepper – instead they had to make do with the cheaper cumin, coriander and ginger. The sale of salt was controlled by the government and this made it expensive. Salt was important for preserving food in a hot climate, and for flavour. Depending on the season of the year, there were fruits such as mangoes, melons, berries and coconuts.

**1** Look at Source A. How can you tell that the zamindar was the most important landholder in the village?

**2** Source B shows an Indian village in 1813. Describe the scene and compare it with a village you know today.

# 5

# The roots of poverty

*India at this time was a country rich in land. This meant that there was plenty of spare land for cultivation if peasants wished to clear it and prepare it for ploughing.*

*Why was there so much poverty if there was plenty of land?*

## Floods and droughts

Too much rain could produce floods, while too little could cause a drought. Both could result in terrible poverty and even famine. Only a few areas had major irrigation works. Most people relied on wells which would dry up during a long drought but when rainfall was heavy (especially during the monsoon rains) there was little anyone could do if the rivers burst their banks and floodwater swept away the crops.

● How do you think drought could lead to famine?

The losses from such catastrophes could be huge: people at the time estimated that the Gujarat famine of 1630–32 caused three million deaths. Between 1702 and 1704, two million people are said to have died from starvation in the Deccan.

● How do some countries today avoid famines even if they have a drought?

Source A  *Two houses near Calcutta in Bengal.*
*Above: a landlord's house. Below: a village hut.*

## Harsh taxes

The Mughal tax system led to great hardship for the peasants. Mughal tax collectors took between 33% and 50% of the value of the peasants' crops.

Everyone hated this, but poor peasants were hardest hit: they were often forced into debt and dependency on others. Mansabdars did not protect the peasants on their lands from the harsh tax system: their incomes came from these taxes and the emperor did not let them keep the same lands for long.

## Source C

François Bernier, a French doctor, describes what happened to peasants who could not pay their taxes.

'These poor people have their surplus [spare money and crops] confiscated and their children carried away as slaves. Sometimes peasants abandon the villages and seek a better life in the towns or camps. Sometimes they run away to territories outside the Mughal Empire.'

F. Bernier, *Travels in the Mogul Empire 1656–1668*

## Source B

Fray Sebastien Manrique, a Catholic missionary, describes the methods used by the mansabdars to extract taxes from the peasants.

'As soon as the mansabdars get power over the peasants, as they have no idea how long they will be able to keep their lands, they at once start to rule by force and violence.

The peasants are first beaten without mercy and maltreated and then sold in the public market as slaves. They are carried off, attached to heavy iron chains, to various markets and fairs, with their poor unhappy wives behind them carrying their small children in their arms, all crying and lamenting their evil plight.'

Hakluyt Society, *Travels of Fray Sebastien Manrique 1629–1643*

● What happens to people in Britain today who try to avoid paying their taxes?

1 Compare the two houses in Source A. Which house do you think would best withstand a flood? Give reasons for your answer.

2 Read Sources B and C. What happened to peasants who did not pay their taxes? Why do you think all peasants did not just run away?

3 Sources B and C were written by Europeans. Does this make them unreliable? Give reasons for your answer.

4 Of the causes of poverty discussed in this unit, which is the most important and which is the least important?

# The lifestyle of the rich

*Under the rule of Akbar's son, Jahangir, and his grandson, Shahjahan, the emperor and richest nobles enjoyed a lavish lifestyle. Some historians believe that the nobles' incomes were the highest in the world at that time.*

*What did the ruling classes spend their money on?*

## Feeding the animals

The Mughal emperors were massive spenders. The estimated daily cost of Shahjahan's food and clothing, together with the cost of feeding the imperial animals, was 50,000 rupees, or about £6,250. There were, it is true, a lot of animals to feed: Shahjahan kept between 200,000 and 300,000 horses at Agra and Delhi, along with 8,000 to 9,000 elephants.

Imperial rules meant that nobles also had to spend lavishly on their stables and military equipment: elephants, camels, mules and carts had to be kept in good condition for the army, and travelling noblemen needed expensive tents made of silk or brocade to stay in. Nobles employed as many as four men to look after each elephant, two or three for each horse, and teams of men to put up their huge tents.

### Source A
***A Mughal nobleman.***
- *How can you tell that he is wealthy?*

## Expensive clothes

The nobles' clothing followed the fashion of the Mughal court. Akbar had 1,000 suits of clothes made up each year, which consisted of expensive cottons and silks made up into undergarments, breeches or tight trousers, shirts, and in winter a vest stuffed with cotton for extra warmth, plus a loose-fitting coat. A turban wrapped around the head, and a shawl round the shoulder or a *patka* (sash) round the waist completed the outfit. From Jahangir's reign it was also fashionable for men to have their ears pierced for earrings, as both men and women wore jewellery.

Rich women's clothes were equally elegant and sometimes of such fine texture that they could be worn only once.

Source B *A Mughal lady.*

## A meal with a hundred courses

Meals could be elaborate affairs: Akbar's friend Abul Fazl was said to have a hundred dishes served whenever he took a meal. Fine fruits were imported from central Asia and Afghanistan, and ice, an item of great luxury in such a hot country, was used by nobles in all seasons. Food was eaten off plates of gold, silver or porcelain, and drinking cups were filled with coffee from Arabia, or with wine or sherbet.

● How do you think the Mughals got their ice?

The Emperor Shahjahan is believed to have spent 30,000 rupees (£3,750) each day on his harem (the women, and their living-quarters). Each noble had three or four wives and each wife had 10, 20 or 100 slaves according to her wealth. The nobles probably spent most of their money on their houses and harems.

---

**1** Study Sources A, B and C. What do they tell you about how rich men and women dressed and lived in Mughal times?

**2** Compare your lifestyle with that of a Mughal nobleman. Who do you think is better off, and why? Include in your answer food, clothing and housing.

---

## Source C

François Bernier, a French doctor, describes the luxury inside a Muslim noble's house.

'Inside a good house the whole floor is covered with a fine cotton mattress four inches in thickness, over which a fine white cloth is spread during the summer, and a silk carpet in the winter. On one side of the room are one or two mattresses, with fine covers decorated with delicate silk embroidery, laced with gold and silver. These are intended for the master of the house, or for important visitors.

Five or six feet from the floor, the sides of the room are full of shelves, in which are seen porcelain vases and flower-pots. The ceiling is gilt and painted, but without pictures of man or beast, such representations being forbidden by the religion of the country [that is, Islam].'

F. Bernier, *Travels in the Mogul Empire, 1656–1668*

# 7

# Roads and rivers

*The demand of the rich for luxury goods was good for business: the Mughals bought silk textiles from Gujarat and precious stones from Goa. The Mughal tax system also encouraged trade as peasants had to sell their produce at market to get the cash to pay their taxes.*

*How were goods transported across India in Mughal times?*

## By land and sea

The maps on this page show the major roads, ports, minerals and industries in India during the seventeenth century. The map on page 4 shows the great size of India – it would be possible to fit Great Britain, for example, into India sixteen times!

*The main roads and ports of India in the seventeenth century.*

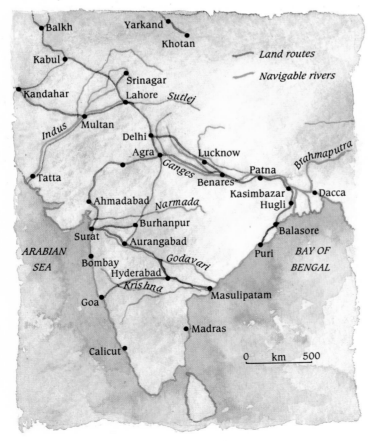

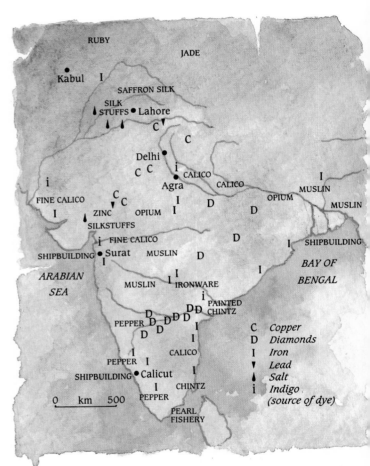

*The main products of India in the seventeenth century.*

Water transport was about a third of the cost of land transport, so many bulky goods were transported by sea. River transport was very slow, particularly when travelling upstream, and parts of many rivers were only navigable at certain times of the year.

The chief means of land transport in India was the light two-wheeled bullock cart. These carts were faster than camels and could carry more; they were also the cheapest form of transport overland for people and goods. But large numbers of camels were kept in western Rajasthan, Gujarat and Sind and were particularly useful in the desert where bullock carts could become stuck in the sand.

## Rivers of mud

Road surfaces often turned into rivers of mud during the monsoon. The Mughal engineers built stone bridges only over the smaller streams. Large rivers could be crossed by bridges made of boats tied together, or more usually by ferries.

Traders rarely travelled alone, and for safety they usually formed large groups known as 'caravans'. Many roads were narrow, and this could lead to disputes and even fighting when two caravans met and could not pass. A traveller might be delayed for two or three days waiting for a large caravan of pack oxen to pass by.

Source A *The 'bridge of boats'. This illustration, from a book dated 1561, called the* Akbarnama, *shows Akbar trying to control an elephant which is chasing another elephant across the collapsing bridge.*

● What sorts of problems do road-users today have to face?

## Places to rest

Conditions were better on the wide imperial highways. These ran between avenues of mulberry trees, and had wells, distance markers and rest-houses (*sarais*) at regular intervals. The best rest-houses could accommodate between 800 and 1,000 people with their horses, camels and carts. They were often built in a square, like cloisters in a monastery, with a courtyard surrounded by rooms, halls and shops. Beds were provided, but travellers had to bring their own bedding. Foreign traders sometimes stayed in them for long periods, paying a monthly rent. Security was usually good, so business could be conducted in safety.

### Source B

Nicolao Manucci describes the security system at a *sarai* which he visited.

'In every sarai is an official whose duty it is to close the gates at dusk … At six o'clock in the morning, before opening the gates, the watchman gives three warnings to the travellers, crying in a loud voice that everyone must look after his own things. After these warnings, if anyone suspects that any of his property is missing, the doors are not opened until the lost thing is found. In this way they catch the thief who is then hanged opposite the sarai.'

N. Manucci, *History of the Moguls, 1653–1708*

---

**1** Make a list of the industries shown on the map opposite.

**2** Choose three of the industries from your list and describe how you would transport the goods to Delhi.

**3** You are an adviser to a Mughal emperor. Suggest how he could improve the transport system in India.

# 8

# A great trading empire

*Under the Mughals, India was probably the world's greatest exporter of textiles. Fine luxury cloth and humbler fabrics were exported to South-east Asia, the Middle East and Europe.*

## Who was involved in overseas trade?

### The power of the merchants of Gujarat

Muslim Indian merchants from Gujarat dominated trade in the Indian Ocean at the beginning of the Mughal period. Gujarati merchants traded Indian cloth in the Red Sea, the Persian Gulf and along the east coast of Africa long before any European ships traded there. Their ships also sailed regularly between Cambay (in Gujarat) and Malacca (in modern Malaya). In Malacca, merchants from India, China and Java met to exchange their goods.

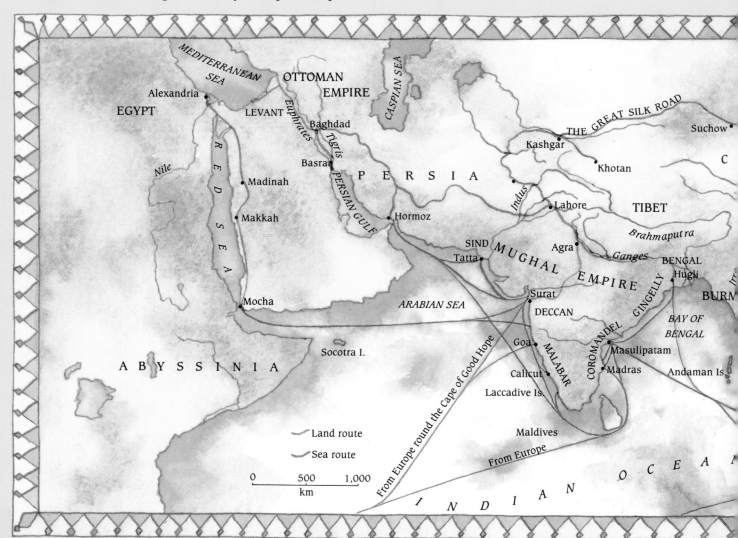

*The great trading empire of the seventeenth century.*

As well as cloth, Gujarati merchants exported rice, pulses, wheat, coconuts, ginger and turmeric to Malacca, Aden and Hormoz. They traded these for silver bullion (solid bars of silver) from the Red Sea and Persian Gulf to make Mughal coins, for horses from Arabia for the Mughal cavalry, and for spices, ivory and dyewoods (woods from which dye can be extracted).

## Enter the Portuguese

The Portuguese were the first Europeans to challenge India's great trade at sea. In 1510 they captured the island of Goa; in 1511 they captured Malacca; and in 1515 they took Hormoz in the Persian Gulf.

The Portuguese capture of Malacca meant that trade between India and South-east Asia was reduced. Gujarati merchants were now forced to share the transport of spices from South-east Asia with the Portuguese. However, the Gujarati merchants were actually able to increase their trade with the Arabs of the Middle East because Portuguese attacks on Arab traders made the Portuguese unwelcome there.

## The Dutch take over

By the end of the seventeenth century, overseas trade had started to slip out of the hands of Indian traders. By then it was the Dutch who were the biggest threat to Indian shipping. During the seventeenth century, the Dutch completely controlled the trade in spices. They forced the Gujarati merchants out of the trade with Indonesia. Gujarati traders concentrated instead on trade with the Middle East. But by the end of the seventeenth century even this trade was in decline.

● The Dutch had a *monopoly* on the trade in spices. Find out what a monopoly is. Can you think of any modern examples of a monopoly?

**1** Study the map in this unit. Make a list of the countries trading with the Mughal Empire.

**2** Find out which places were conquered by the Portuguese between 1510 and 1515. How would these conquests have helped the Portuguese to become wealthy traders in India during the sixteenth century? Explain your answer carefully.

**3** What caused the decline of the Gujarati merchant traders?

# 9

# Mughal towns and cities

*The Mughal period was a golden age for the growth of towns and cities in India. Many remains of these beautiful cities can still be seen today.*

*Were the Mughal towns and cities as splendid as their remains suggest?*

### The towns grow

As many as sixteen to seventeen million people (15 per cent of the population) lived in towns and cities in India by the seventeenth century. In England at that time, 13 per cent of the population was to be found in towns. Nine Indian cities had populations of 200,000 or more, including Delhi, Agra and Surat. In the whole of Europe at that time there were only three cities with such large populations – London, Paris and Naples.

### Why did the towns grow?

There were several reasons for the growth of towns during the Mughal period.

Peace was brought to a large part of India by the Mughal Empire. This helped trade and led to the development of larger towns where goods could be bought and sold. The growth of trade led especially to the expansion of the textile industry, which was concentrated in towns.

Market towns were also developing as a result of the Mughal policy to collect taxes in cash. This forced the peasants to travel to market to sell their produce. As a result, towns became important centres for trade and commerce.

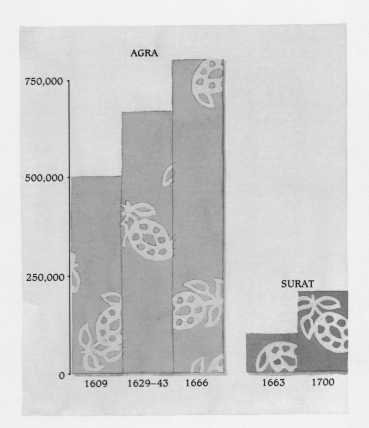

**Source A** *Some estimates of town population in Mughal India.*

**Source B** *Modern picture of the Red Fort at Agra.*

## Splendid new buildings and towns

Mughal emperors also founded completely new towns and cities. Shahjahan built a new capital city, in 1648, which today is known as Old Delhi. Indeed the Mughal emperors created some of the most magnificent architecture in the world to show off the wealth and splendour of their empire.

Akbar was responsible for much impressive architecture, including the Red Fort at Agra (Source B). In 1571 he decided to build a new imperial capital city and for the next fourteen years the stone-masons laboured to create a great new palace and city which was called Fatehpur Sikri (*fatehpur* means 'victory').

Today the complete palace still stands, looking as if it had been built only yesterday and not 400 years ago. But it is a deserted, ghostly place, and all that remains of the town that once surrounded the palace is an outer defensive wall.

Source C    *The building of the Red Fort at Agra. The fort was built of red sandstone. Akbar had his capital at Agra, and the fort was constructed between 1565 and 1570.*

● *Compare the Mughal picture of the building of Agra with the modern photograph of the Red Fort. What differences can you see?*

**Source D** *The Taj Mahal. This exquisite tomb was built by the Emperor Shahjahan in memory of his beloved wife, Mumtaz Mahal. The skilled craftsmen who built it came from all over the Islamic world, including the dome builder who came from Turkey.*

## The Taj Mahal

Between 1632 and 1648 the world-famous tomb, the Taj Mahal at Agra, was created by the Emperor Shahjahan. It was built in memory of his wife Mumtaz Mahal who died in 1631 while giving birth to her fourteenth child.

- Find out what the seven wonders of the world were. How many are still standing today?

## Source E

Jean-Baptiste Tavernier, a French jewel-merchant, describes the building of the Taj Mahal.

'I witnessed the start and completion of this great work, which took 22 years to complete, during which 22,000 men worked incessantly. This helps one to realise that the cost has been enormous. It is said that the scaffolding alone cost more than the building itself: because there was a shortage of wood, the scaffolding and the supports of the arches had all to be made of brick; this has meant a great deal of work and expense.'

J.-B. Tavernier, *Travels in India*, 1676

## Source F

François Bernier, a French doctor, compares the Taj Mahal with the pyramids in Egypt.

'This building is a vast dome of white marble … The centre of every arch is decorated with white marble on which are inscribed large arabian characters in black marble, which produce a fine effect. Everywhere are seen the jasper, or jade, as well as other stones of great value and rarity, set in an endless variety of ways in the slabs of marble which face the wall …

I decidedly think that this monument deserves much more to be numbered among the wonders of the world than the pyramids of Egypt …'

F. Bernier, *Travels in the Mogul Empire, 1656–1668*

## Source G

Jean-Baptiste Tavernier comments on the state of Lahore, a city in modern Pakistan.

'The town is large, and extends more than two miles in length, but the greater part of the houses, which are higher than those of Agra and Delhi, are falling into ruins, the excessive rains having demolished a large number.'

J.-B. Tavernier, *Travels in India*, 1676

## Source H   *The city of Patna, during the nineteenth century.*

● *What does this picture tell us about many of the buildings in Mughal cities?*

## Source I

François Bernier comments on housing in Delhi.

'In among these different houses is an immense number of small ones, built of mud and thatched with straw, in which live the common people, and all that great number of servants and camp-followers who follow the court and the army.

It is as a result of these thatched cottages that Delhi has such frequent fires. More than sixty thousand roofs were destroyed by three fires during the last windy season. So rapid were the flames that several camels and horses and poor women were burnt.'

F. Bernier, *Travels in the Mogul Empire*, 1656–1668

---

**1** Study Source A. What evidence is there that towns grew during the seventeenth century?

**2** Study Sources D, E and F. Write your own description of the Taj Mahal as if you were a guide with a party of tourists.

**3** In Source F, Bernier says that the Taj should be numbered among the wonders of the world. Do you think he was right? Explain your answer.

**4** Study Sources G, H and I. What impression do they give of Mughal cities?

**5** In what way is the impression of Mughal cities given in Sources G, H and I different from that gained from previous sources?

**6** How do you explain the fact that the sources in this unit give contradictory impressions of Mughal cities?

# 10

# Shivaji: the challenge of the 'Mountain Rat'

*Aurangzeb was the last of the great Mughal emperors. His reign saw both the expansion of the Mughal Empire to its greatest size, and the start of its decline. The first big challenge to Aurangzeb came from a powerful local chief called Shivaji.*

*Was Shivaji a bandit or a freedom fighter?*

**A threat to the great Mughal Empire**

Shivaji was a Maratha chieftain. The Marathas were Hindu people who lived in the Deccan.

In 1663, Shivaji attacked and humiliated Aurangzeb's deputy in the Deccan. Then in 1664 Shivaji, who was a Hindu, seized and looted the port of Surat, which was used by Muslim pilgrims on their way to the holy city of Makkah, in Arabia.

Shivaji was then captured and imprisoned by the Emperor in Agra. In 1666 the 'Mountain Rat', as he was known at the Mughal court, tricked the guards and managed to escape from captivity. He returned to the Deccan, where he gradually built up a large area of land for the Marathas. By the time he died in 1680, he controlled his own small state, independent of the Mughals.

**Source A**  *The Maratha chief, Shivaji.*
*A miniature portrait painted about 1680. On his right hand is a gauntlet (an armoured glove).*

## Source B

Khafi Khan, a Muslim historian of Aurangzeb's time, writes about Shivaji.

'Whenever Shivaji came to know of a populated and rich town he attacked it, robbed its people and took it into his possession ... He collected a large number of selected robbers from among the Marathas and prepared to capture the well-known Mughal strong forts ...'

Khafi Khan, *History of Alamgir*, about 1680

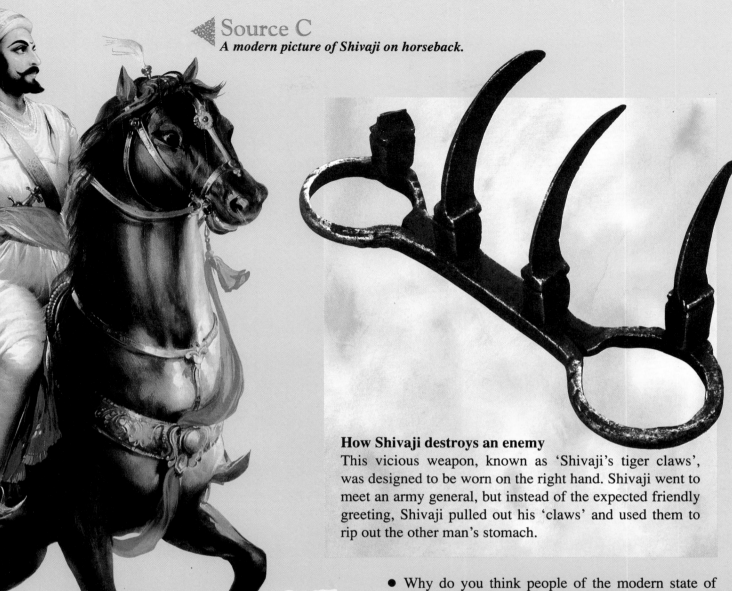

## Source C

*A modern picture of Shivaji on horseback.*

**How Shivaji destroys an enemy**

This vicious weapon, known as 'Shivaji's tiger claws', was designed to be worn on the right hand. Shivaji went to meet an army general, but instead of the expected friendly greeting, Shivaji pulled out his 'claws' and used them to rip out the other man's stomach.

● Why do you think people of the modern state of Maharashtra still look upon Shivaji as a hero?

## Source D

An Indian nationalist, writing in 1900, looks back at Maratha power with pride.

'The rise of Maratha power was due to the upheaval of the whole [Maratha] population, strongly bound together by their similar languages, race, religion and literature ... This was the first experiment of its kind attempted in India after the disastrous period of foreign Muslim [Mughal] invasions ... It was a national movement or upheaval in which all classes of people co-operated.'

M. G. Ranade, *Rise of the Maratha Power,* 1900

1 Look at Source A. Does this fit with the Mughal view that Shivaji was a mountain rat?

2 Read Source B. What evidence is there that Shivaji was a 'bandit' or a 'rebel'?

3 Study Sources C and D. What sort of impression do they give of Shivaji?

4 Sources C and D were produced a long time after Shivaji's death. How do you explain the fact that these sources, produced a long time after the event, contradict Source B, which was written during Aurangzeb's reign?

# 11

# Aurangzeb: your verdict?

*Aurangzeb conquered many new lands for the Mughal Empire. During his reign it reached its greatest extent. But he also faced problems. The Maratha revolt, led by Shivaji, drew the Emperor Aurangzeb into a long war in the south of India. And he saw the wealth of the empire drain away.*

*Was Aurangzeb a good ruler?*

## An expanding empire

Look again at the map on page 7. Aurangzeb successfully conquered part of the Deccan between 1686 and 1687. But he was not satisfied with these victories. He kept all the best lands for himself and used the taxes from them to continue the war further south. This annoyed some nobles who had expected to be given these lands as a reward for their support.

## Raids and rebellions

Elsewhere in the empire, Aurangzeb's enemies made the most of his problems in the south of India. In 1669 and 1685 people in the region south of Delhi rebelled against the high Mughal taxes. In the 1670s, Aurangzeb also faced rebellions from peasants to the west of Delhi and the Sikhs in the north, as well as raids from people in the border areas of north-west India.

**Source A**  *Aurangzeb on horseback in about 1680.*

## Source B

A modern historian sums up Aurangzeb's achievement.

'In less than ten years, Aurangzeb was able to conquer Bijapur and Golconda as well as the lands of the Marathas. Never in the history of the subcontinent had a single monarch ruled over a vaster area.

He spent the remaining seventeen years of his life in trying to consolidate the territories which he had conquered for his Empire.'

S. Moinul Haq, *History of Alamgir*, 1975

## Muslims first

Finally, Aurangzeb abandoned the Mughal policy of religious toleration. Earlier emperors such as Akbar had been careful to treat people of all religions very fairly. Aurangzeb, who was a very strict Muslim, had a different policy. He demolished Hindu temples in Jodhpur, for example, and promoted Muslims to high positions in areas where Hindus had rebelled. He tried to replace Hindus with Muslims in his civil service. He also re-introduced the poll tax or *jizya* on non-Muslims. This tax had been abolished by Akbar a hundred years earlier.

## Source D

Nicolao Manucci, an Italian gunner and 'quack' doctor, questions the benefits of Aurangzeb's rule.

'Aurangzeb says, "My subjects are able to enjoy in peace and with delight all the benefits my rule has produced. My kingdom is now full of noble mosques instead of the hideous temples crowded with idols. Instead of taverns and brothels, which would have spread their poison all around, we find congregations of holy men, modest and full of wisdom, who proclaim the greatness of God."

But despite what Aurangzeb says, it is undeniable that in India every day there are committed the most monstrous crimes in the world.'

N. Manucci, *History of the Moguls 1653–1708*

## Source E   *Badshahi Mosque, Lahore.*
*Aurangzeb had many new mosques built during his reign.*

## Source C

Aurangzeb's court historian praises his ruler's religious activities and his belief in the teachings of Islam.

'Aurangzeb keeps the fasts on Fridays and other sacred days and he reads the Friday prayers with the common people. He fasts during the whole month of Ramadan [a period of daylight fasting in the Mughal calendar], says the prayers appointed for the month and reads the Holy Qur'an. He refrains from forbidden meats, does not listen to music, and does not wear prohibited clothes or use vessels of gold or silver. In his sacred court no wicked talk, no word of backbiting or lie is allowed.'

Mohammed Kazim, *Alamgırnama [History of Aurangzeb]*, about 1668

---

1 Which sources in this unit suggest that Aurangzeb was a holy ruler? Why might some people describe his behaviour as that of a religious fanatic? Would such a label be fair?

2 What evidence from this unit could you use to show that Aurangzeb was a far-sighted statesman?

3 What evidence from this unit could you use to show that Aurangzeb was over-ambitious, and tried to extend his empire too far?

4 Using all the evidence in this unit, do you think Aurangzeb was a good ruler?

# The decline of the Mughals

*By the eighteenth century, local rulers in India had grown in power.*
*They were no longer prepared to obey the Mughal emperors.*

*Why did local rulers emerge? What effect did they have?*

## Power passes away from the Mughals

Why did local rulers grow in power?

In the twelve years after Aurangzeb's death in 1707, there were ten emperors. Because there was weakness at the top, local rulers in the provinces became more ambitious.

The practice of moving *mansabdars* (rank-holding officers) around every few years had stopped. Local rulers were now able to build up a large personal following and they passed on their power and wealth to their sons.

By the eighteenth century, local rulers were tempted to send only small amounts of the tax to the emperor, pocketing the rest for themselves.

## Chaos and plunder

In 1739 the Persian ruler, Nadir Shah, sacked the city of Delhi. He returned home with an enormous treasure worth £30 million, including the famous Koh-i-Noor diamond. This very large Indian diamond was later taken by the British and became part of the Crown Jewels.

Between 1748 and 1761 the Afghans under Ahmed Shah Durrani invaded north India four times. In the winter of 1756–57 Delhi was turned into a nightmare city of rape, plunder and massacre. Only the Marathas had the power to stop the Afghan raiders. In 1761 the Marathas fought the Afghan invaders at the third battle of Panipat.

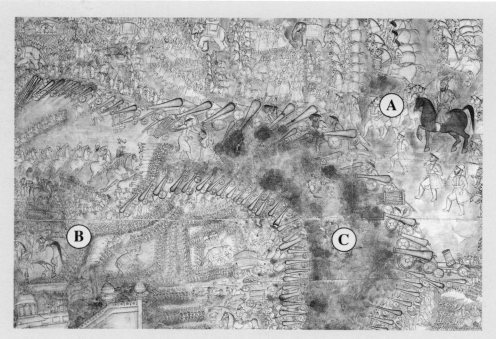

Source A **The Battle of Panipat, 1761.** *Ahmed Shah Durrani, (A) the Afghan king and victor, is on the chestnut horse on the right. On the left, the defeated Maratha general (B) is helped from his horse. The cannons of the two armies (C) face each other near the centre.*

## Massacre at Panipat

The Afghans, who were Muslims, called for a *jihad* (a holy war) against the Hindu Marathas. This made it impossible for the Marathas to buy food from the Muslim population living near Panipat. With their men and horses starving, the Marathas had to abandon their strong defensive position and face the great guns of the Afghans. The result was a massacre: 75,000 Marathas were slaughtered and 30,000 taken prisoner and later ransomed.

The Marathas' power in north India went into decline. The Afghan army returned home. Neither the Mughals nor the Marathas were now strong in north India. This helped the British to expand into this region.

Short-lived emperors

No-one dares tell _me_ what to do.

Regional states

INDUS
Chenab
Sutlej
TIBET
NEPAL
RAJPUTS
Jumna
Ganges
Brahmaputra
MARATHA
BENGAL
TERRITORY
Narmada
ARABIAN SEA
BAY OF BENGAL
MARATHAS
Godavari
Krishna
MYSORE
CEYLON

The decline of Mughal power

Rise of local rulers

The local rulers are not handing over the money.

Invasion of Persians and Afghans

Shortage of money

**1** Explain in your own words why local rulers grew in power in India during the eighteenth century.

**2** How many reasons can you find to explain the decline in Mughal power?

**3** Use Source A to help you explain how the battle of Panipat was fought and won.

The East India Company was set up in 1600 in the reign of Elizabeth I. It traded with the East Indies (modern South-east Asia). During the seventeenth and eighteenth centuries, the East India Company increased its trade with India. It traded silver for fine Indian silks and cotton cloth.

By the middle of the eighteenth century, the East India Company had its own army to protect its valuable trade in India. In 1757, the East India Company army won a victory at the battle of Plassey. This led to the conquest of Bengal. The East India Company army also defeated Tipu Sultan of Mysore (1799) and the Marathas (1818).

As the East India Company took over more and more of India, it appointed Governor-Generals to rule. Governor-General Bentinck introduced a law against widow burning (*sati*) in 1829.

In 1857, many Indians rebelled against the British rule. The rebellion was so serious that the East India Company was abolished. In 1858 the British Crown became the new ruler in India. Queen Victoria was proclaimed Empress of India in 1877.

# British power

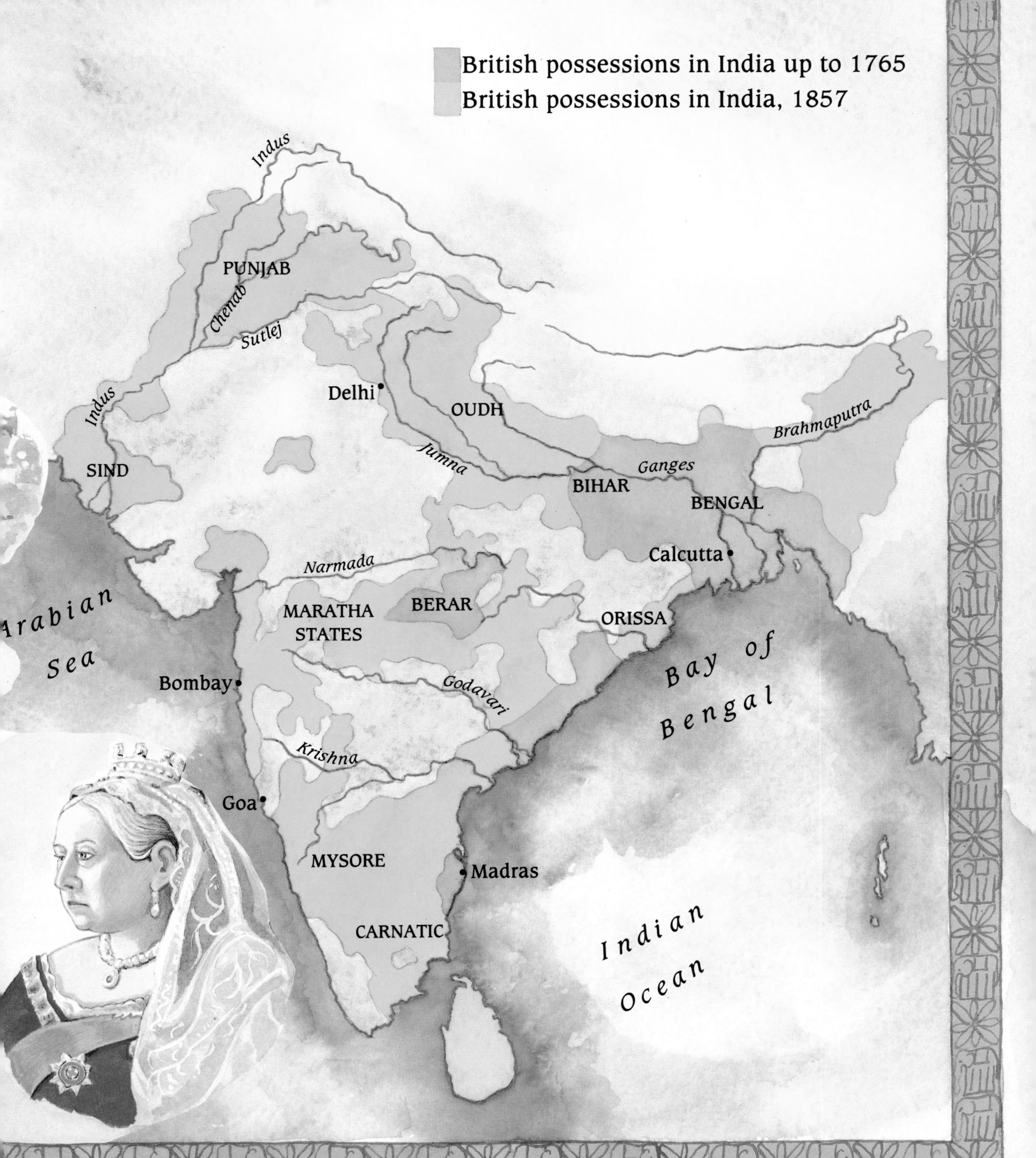

British possessions in India up to 1765
British possessions in India, 1857

*Indus*

PUNJAB

*Chenab*

*Sutlej*

*Indus*

Delhi

OUDH

*Brahmaputra*

SIND

*Jumna*

*Ganges*

BIHAR

BENGAL

Calcutta

*Narmada*

MARATHA
STATES

BERAR

ORISSA

*Godavari*

*Bay of
Bengal*

*Arabian
Sea*

Bombay

*Krishna*

Goa

MYSORE

Madras

CARNATIC

*Indian
Ocean*

# 13

# The British in Bengal

*There was nothing inevitable about the growth of British power in India. Powerful local rulers in India like Siraj-ud-Daula in Bengal tried to stop British expansion.*

## Why did the British conquer Bengal?

### The East India Company

In the seventeenth and early eighteenth centuries the British went to India to trade silver for fine Indian silk and cotton cloth. The risks involved in trade with Asia were thought to be too great for individual merchants. Because it was so risky, the East India Company was set up as a *joint stock company*. This meant that merchants pooled their resources to help each other rather than risk trading alone. The English East India Company was founded in 1600 with 219 members.

Until the 1740s, the Company and its Court of Directors in London were only interested in trading. But gradually during the eighteenth century, the Company had to pay for its own private army to protect its trade in India. The fear that French power might grow in India made the Company expand its army quickly. By the end of the eighteenth century the Company controlled one of the largest armies in the world.

***Modern-day Calcutta.*** *Before the British arrived, Calcutta was just a small village on the banks of the Hooghly river. Today it is the second largest city in India.*

● *How has Calcutta changed since 1754 (Source A)*

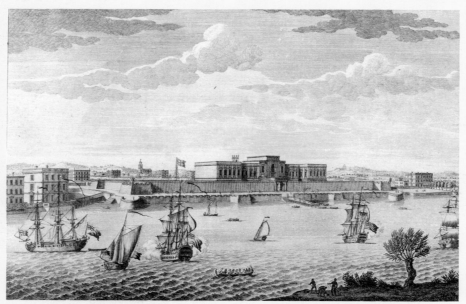

### Why did the British take control of Bengal?

Calcutta was founded by the East India Company as a trading station in 1690. By 1760 it had a population of about 100,000. Fine Bengali cloth was purchased by Company servants in the Calcutta region and there were many opportunities for trade up the Ganges and Jumna rivers.

Source A   ***Fort William at Calcutta.*** *An engraving by a Dutch artist in 1754.*

38

Some British traders wanted more power in Bengal. They believed they could make more money if they got rid of rich Indian merchants who controlled much of the trade. But there were no British plans to take over Bengal until a crisis in 1756–57.

## Crisis in Calcutta

In 1756 the new young ruler of Bengal, Siraj-ud-Daula, attacked and took over Calcutta. He believed that the growth of Calcutta and British trade was a threat to his power. He was made suspicious by the British move to fortify Calcutta. He had also been insulted by the Company's failure to send him the usual presents when he became ruler earlier in 1756.

## Winning back Calcutta

The British Lieutenant-Colonel, Robert Clive, was sent from Madras to recapture Calcutta. On arriving there, Clive learnt that Siraj had other enemies as well as the British: better-off farmers hated Siraj's endless demands for tax, and the immensely rich Indian bankers did not trust him. Clive chose to side with these powerful people against the unpopular Siraj. A plot was hatched on 4 June 1756. It was agreed that Mir Jafar, one of Siraj-ud-Daula's military commanders, would not lead his forces into battle against the British. In return, Mir Jafar would become the next ruler of Bengal.

## The battle of Plassey, 1757

Clive then moved his forces to Plassey. The famous battle of Plassey was little more than a skirmish. There was some exchange of gunfire. But it had been agreed beforehand by the plotters that the bulk of Siraj's army under Mir Jafar would not fight. Once the rest of Siraj's army saw that they had been tricked, they left with little bloodshed. Siraj himself was captured and killed by the conspirators.

**Source B**  *Siraj-ud-Daula, the new ruler of Bengal in 1756.*

**Source C**  *Robert Clive, his opponent at Calcutta.*

**Source D** *Robert Clive meets Mir Jafar after the battle of Plassey.* *This was painted in about 1761 by a British artist. Mir Jafar was now ruler of Bengal, but was actually under British control.*

### Robert Clive: a wealthy man

Although only a skirmish, the battle of Plassey signalled a revolution. The British were now able to establish complete control over the rulers of Bengal. They were to make huge profits from this, the richest province in India.

Clive gained an immediate personal fortune of £234,000. He was made a mansabdar, and received lands south of Calcutta worth £30,000 a year. Overnight, at the age of 32, he became one of Britain's wealthiest men.

● *How have the two men been shown by the artist?*

1 Why did the East India Company recruit its own private army?

2 What clues does Source A provide as to why Siraj-ud-Daula might fear the British?

3 Make a list of the reasons for the British conquest of Bengal. Identify which were short-term and which were long-term causes.

4 Look at Source D. Do the British or the Indians appear more powerful? Explain your answer carefully.

# 14

# The Black Hole of Calcutta

*In 1756 Siraj, the ruler of Bengal, attacked Calcutta. His soldiers held a number of British prisoners overnight in a small room at Fort William. This cell was known as the Black Hole. The prisoners' leader was called John Holwell. Later he claimed that most of the British prisoners died of suffocation in this dungeon.*

**What really happened in the Black Hole of Calcutta?**

**Source A** *The barracks at Fort William. The Black Hole was behind the barred windows on the left. This is an artist's imaginary view, drawn in 1882.*

## Source B

John Holwell describes the night spent in the Black Hole.

'Of 146 prisoners, 123 were smothered in the Black-Hole prison in the night of 20 June 1756 ... From about nine till near eleven ... my legs were almost broke with the weight against them. By the time I was very nearly pressed to death ... I travelled over the dead and went to the other end of the room ...

The moment I moved from the window my breathing grew short and painful ... I was seized with a pain in my breast and palpitation of my heart ... I had, in a fit of thirst, attempted drinking my urine, but it was so intensely bitter, there was no enduring a second taste ...

From half past eleven till nearly two in the morning, I sustained the weight of a heavy man, with his knees in my back, and the pressure of his whole body on my head.'

Holwell's *Genuine Narrative*, February 1757

41

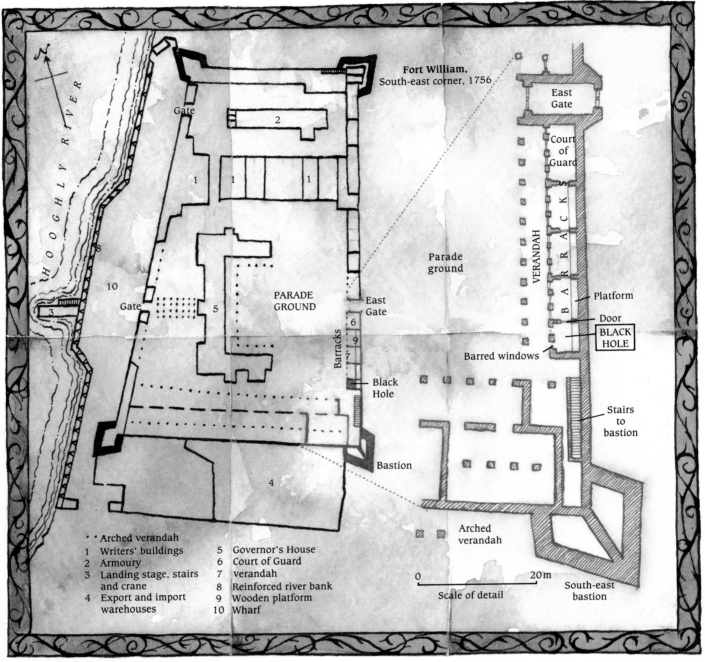

**Plan of Fort William in Calcutta, showing the position of the Black Hole.**

Fort William, South-east corner, 1756

East Gate

Court of Guard

Platform

Door

BLACK HOLE

Barred windows

VERANDAH

BARRACKS

Parade ground

Stairs to bastion

Arched verandah

South-east bastion

HOOGHLY RIVER

Gate

2

1   1   1

Gate

5

PARADE GROUND

Barracks

East Gate

6

9

7

Black Hole

Bastion

4

3

8

10

• • Arched verandah
1   Writers' buildings
2   Armoury
3   Landing stage, stairs and crane
4   Export and import warehouses
5   Governor's House
6   Court of Guard
7   verandah
8   Reinforced river bank
9   Wooden platform
10  Wharf

0                    20m
Scale of detail

● *Can you see where Source A is on the plan?*

## Source C

A modern historian questions Holwell's story.

'At six o'clock in the morning, Holwell was found "under the dead", but the fresh air instantly revived him. The whole night which claimed the lives of 123 persons, if Holwell is to be relied upon, had only temporary effects on him. The same day of his release from the dungeon he walked three miles, and the next day, in spite of the boils that covered him from head to foot, he marched the same distance with heavy fetters, and "under the scorching beams of an intense hot sun".'

B. K. Gupta, *Sirajuddaula and the East India Company*, 1962

## Source D

Lord Curzon, the British ruler of India from 1899 to 1904, unveils a memorial to the people who died in the Black Hole.

'If among those builders of Empire there are any who especially deserve commemoration, surely it is the martyr band whose fate I recall and whose names I revive on this site. If there be a spot that should be dear to an Englishman in India, it is that below our feet, which was stained with the blood and which closed over the remains of the victims of that night of 20 June 1756.'

Lord Curzon's speech when unveiling the new Black-Hole memorial, 19 December 1902

## Source E

Subash Chandra Bose, an Indian nationalist who did not want the British to be in India, campaigns to pull down the Black-Hole memorial in 1940.

'The campaign against this monument has to be taken up at once. The 3rd of July 1940 is going to be observed in Bengal as the Siraj-ud-Daula Day – in honour of the last independent king of Bengal. The monument is not just an unwarranted stain on the memory of Siraj, but has stood in the heart of Calcutta for the last 150 years or more as the symbol of our slavery and humiliation.'

S. C. Bose, in *Forward Bloc*, 29 June 1940

## Source F

A modern historian concludes that Holwell exaggerated his story.

'It is safe to say that at the most only 64 persons were confined in the Black Hole, of which 21 survived. The area of the room, which was 18 feet by 14 feet and 10 inches, amounted to 267 square feet, giving about 4.2 square feet to each person. This area seems sufficient for a person to stand and sit down, though not without discomfort.'

B. K. Gupta, *Sirajuddaula and the East India Company*, 1962

## Source G

*John Holwell supervises the building of a monument to those who died in Calcutta.* By *an unknown artist.*

---

**1** Look at Source A and at the plan of Fort William. Describe where the Black Hole was and what it was like.

**2** What evidence is there in Source B that the survivors of the Black Hole were heroes?

**3** Can you find any other source in this unit which supports the idea that the Black Hole victims were heroes or martyrs?

**4** How does the historian in Sources C and F cast doubt on the truthfulness of Holwell's story?

**5** Why do you think the modern historian disagrees with Holwell's account?

**6** How would you explain the fact that the author of Source E wanted to pull down the Holwell monument?

**7** Using information from all the sources in this unit, what do you think happened in the Black Hole of Calcutta?

# Tipu Sultan of Mysore

*Tipu Sultan of Mysore challenged British power by developing a new state and an army that could defeat the British.*

**Was Tipu Sultan a cruel tyrant? Or was he an Indian patriot?**

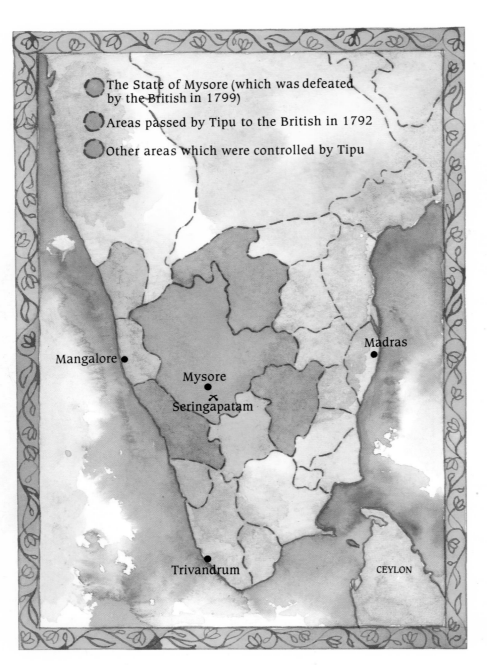

The State of Mysore (which was defeated by the British in 1799)

Areas passed by Tipu to the British in 1792

Other areas which were controlled by Tipu

Mangalore

Madras

Mysore

Seringapatam

Trivandrum

CEYLON

## Mysore: a modern state

Tipu turned Mysore into a strong and wealthy state by introducing new crops and industries. He started the manufacture of silk in Mysore, and set up several weapons factories that could make European-style weapons. He encouraged the cultivation of fine white sugar, betel (the leaf of a plant which is chewed by people in parts of South-east Asia), sandalwood, and hardwood for his navy.

He also had an experimental garden to try out new crops such as pineapples from South Africa, and avocados from Mexico, as well as indigo and cotton plants. The British Governor-General Cornwallis described Mysore as 'a garden from one end to the other'.

To prevent his state being encircled by the British, Tipu tried to gain permanent access to the Indian Ocean in the west. He also tried to stimulate trade across the ocean with Arabia and Persia to help revive Indian shipping.

## Armed for war

A strong economy made possible a strong army. Tipu fought four wars against the British, and in the first two, in 1769 and 1781–84, he was successful. He recruited a multinational army including Afghan cavalrymen, and infantry from Arabia and Abyssinia (modern Ethiopia). The Beda people from the Mysore hills provided sappers, miners and marksmen. Rockets, hand guns and field guns were all made in Mysore, and Tipu also had a huge bullock park of 250,000 white Deccan cattle, which were used to transport field guns and supplies.

## Tipu Sultan: a feared ruler

The British feared and hated the sultan of Mysore. The British called Tipu 'a cruel tyrant' and 'monster', whose treatment of prisoners was inhuman. The British claimed that Tipu was a Muslim fanatic. In fact Tipu made offerings in the Christian churches and the Hindu temples of his loyal subjects; he only destroyed the places of worship of his enemies!

### Source B
A British colonel's view of Tipu:

'The main features of his character were vanity and arrogance: according to Tipu, no human being was ever so handsome, so wise, so learned or so brave as himself. He murdered his English prisoners because he hated their bravery. He oppressed and insulted his Hindu subjects, because he hated their religion. Tipu's court and army was one vast scene of corruption.'

Colonel M. Wilks, *Historical Sketches of the South of India*, 1810

### Source C
*Quilted fabric body armour, sword and helmet for Tipu Sultan. Mysore, late 18th-century.*

### Source A
**Tipu Sultan** *ruled Mysore from 1782 until his death at the battle of Seringapatam in 1799. This portrait was painted in Mysore in 1790.*

Source D *Two of Tipu's sons, aged 10 and 8, are handed over to Lord Cornwallis as hostages. This was painted by a British artist in about 1793.*

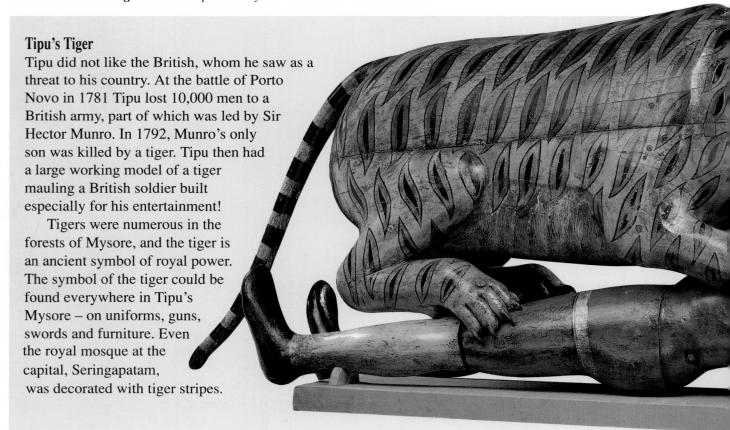

### Tipu's Tiger

Tipu did not like the British, whom he saw as a threat to his country. At the battle of Porto Novo in 1781 Tipu lost 10,000 men to a British army, part of which was led by Sir Hector Munro. In 1792, Munro's only son was killed by a tiger. Tipu then had a large working model of a tiger mauling a British soldier built especially for his entertainment!

Tigers were numerous in the forests of Mysore, and the tiger is an ancient symbol of royal power. The symbol of the tiger could be found everywhere in Tipu's Mysore – on uniforms, guns, swords and furniture. Even the royal mosque at the capital, Seringapatam, was decorated with tiger stripes.

## Tipu's defeat

During the 1790s, the British adopted a far more aggressive attitude in India. The East India Company was no longer just a trading company. It now believed that its future could only be safe if it won full *political* control of India.

During the Third Mysore War, in 1792, the British Governor-General Cornwallis defeated Tipu at Seringapatam. Tipu was forced to pay the Company an indemnity (compensation) of more than 33 million rupees (between £3 million and £4 million), hand over half his territories and all his prisoners, and give two of his sons as hostages.

## The collapse of Mysore

By this time, the Company army was one of the largest armies in the world, with 155,000 soldiers. The British Governor-General in India, and Richard Wellesley and his brother Arthur (later the Duke of Wellington), ordered improvements in the training and equipment of the army and strengthened the cavalry which previously had not been a match for strong Indian cavalry forces.

*'Tipu's Tiger'. Turning the handle on the tiger's side makes the tiger roar and the man scream. It was made of wood in about 1792.*

The final collapse of Mysore came in 1799: Tipu had been unable to gain help from Napoleon of France and several of his commanders deserted him. Tipu was killed on 4 May 1799 at Seringapatam and was buried the next day with full military honours.

## Source E

Tipu wrote to the French in April 1797.

'If you will help me, in a short time not an Englishman will remain in India. You have the power and the means to get rid of the English. Together we will purge India of these cursed villains.'

Quoted in Kabir Kauser, *Secret Correspondence of Tipu Sultan*, 1980

## Source F

Governor-General Wellesley wrote in August 1798:

'Tipu has devised a plan to totally destroy us, and he has prepared his forces for a war of extermination against us. He has also sought the help of our old enemy France.'

R. M. Martin, *Despatches, minutes and correspondence of the Marquis of Wellesley*, 1836–37

---

**1** Look at Source A. Do you think it was painted by an Indian or a British artist? Give reasons for your answer.

**2** Why do you think the symbol of the tiger was so widely used in Tipu's Mysore?

**3** Study carefully the text in this unit. Why do you think the British decided to conquer Mysore? Discuss this question in a group and then list your reasons in order of importance.

**4** Study Source D. How does this source portray the British treatment of hostages? Why would Cornwallis wish to be portrayed in this way?

**5** Some people say that Tipu was an Indian hero, others that he was a cruel dictator. How can you explain these different views?

# 16

# A meeting of two cultures

*For most of the eighteenth century in India Englishmen had Indian wives and mixed socially with Indians. But during the nineteenth century, racial attitudes hardened.*

*Why did British attitudes towards Indians change?*

## The Englishman and his Indian family

**Source A** *William Palmer, his two Indian wives, two of his sons, one daughter, and three other women. The picture was painted by Francesco Renaldi in 1786.*

● *What reasons might these Indian princesses have had for marrying an Englishman?*

## Source B

**Some Englishmen working as Company servants lived with Indian women rather than English wives. A modern historian explains why.**

'In one area of domestic life, relations between the British and Indians were extremely close. British men were in the habit of setting up *zenaras* (harems) and living with Indian women. These women were known as *bibis*, Indian wives. Formal marriages were rare, but men and women lived together as husband and wife, having children and raising families. They were in fact married in all but name …

Marriage with a young woman from Britain was so expensive that few of the Company servants could afford it. British wives required carriages, dressmakers, hairdressers, ladies' maids and nannies. Any children had to be sent to school in England, the mother usually accompanying them.

Captain Thomas Williamson, who went to Bengal as a cadet in 1778 and who retired as a captain in 1796, estimated the cost of keeping a wife in India at £300 per year and the cost of sending one child to England at £150.'

S. Ashton, *The British In India: From Trade to Empire*, 1987

## Source C

Thomas Williamson, who worked for the East India Company, suggests some of the costs of looking after an Indian wife.

'A certain sum to be paid monthly; the pay of two, or three, female servants; an allowance for betel [a leaf which is chewed by many people in India], tobacco (it is very rarely they chew it), shoes, clothes and gold and silver ornaments … Taking a broad outline, we may put down the whole at about forty rupees monthly; equal to sixty pounds sterling per annum.'

T. Williamson, *The East India Vade Mecum*, 1818

**Dancing girls**

## Source D
*A British officer enjoys a nautch, and smokes a **hookah** (water pipe). This picture was painted in about 1820.*

## Source F

A modern historian, Percival Spear, describes how the British ruler, Cornwallis, did not allow Indians to serve in higher-ranking jobs in the East India Company. Indians were only allowed to do the humbler, menial tasks.

'Cornwallis had a strong sense of Indian shortcomings. "Every native of India, I believe," he wrote, "is corrupt." His view of his own countrymen in India was not very different, but whereas he saw a cure for them he could see none at the time for Indians.

So all high Indian officials were dismissed and all posts worth more than £500 a year reserved for Europeans. This measure marked the Company's service with an indelibly foreign stamp, and its effects were felt right down to 1947.'

P. Spear, *A History of India*, 1965

## Source E

Alexander Mackrabie, Sheriff of Calcutta in the 1770s, writes after watching a *nautch*, a display of dancing by professional dancing girls.

'Last night I supped at the house of a Gentleman who has been two months persuading me to see a girl dance. You have heard and read of the Indian dancing girls … There was one principal girl who has a thousand graceful airs and a deal of expression.'

*Mackrabie Journal*, 1775

## Source G  *Government House, Calcutta, built in 1805. This is where the Governor-Generals of India lived before 1857. From a painting by a British artist in about 1819.*

● *What impression of the British would Government House have presented to the Indians as they passed by?*

## Source H

An anonymous writer describes the racial attitudes of a white family in India.

'The married couple become a bundle of English prejudices and hate the country, the natives and everything belonging to them ... The wife's cries of "odious blacks", or "nasty heathen wretches", and "filthy creatures" are the shrill echoes of the "black brutes", and "black vermin" of the husband. The children pick up this language: I have heard one 5 years old, call the man who was taking care of him a "black brute".'

Quoted in P. Spear, *The Nabobs*, 1932

## Source I

Lord Hastings, Governor-General from 1813 to 1823, comments on Hindus.

'The Hindu appears a being nearly limited to mere animal functions ... with no higher intellect than a dog, an elephant, or a monkey.'

October 1813

1 Study Sources A, B and C. Why do you think Englishmen in India during the eighteenth century often preferred to marry Indian rather than English women?

2 Look at Sources D and E. What evidence is there in these sources that race relations in the eighteenth century were often good?

3 What evidence is there in Source F that during the 1790s the Company's attitude to race relations began to change?

4 Does Source G support or contradict Source F? Explain your answer carefully.

5 Study Sources H and I. What evidence can you find to show that race relations between the British and Indians had grown worse by the nineteenth century?

# 17

# Sati: death on the flames

*Between 1828 and 1835 Lord William Bentinck was Governor-General in India. He believed that good laws made good people. One of his most famous laws was the abolition of sati in 1829.*

*How were Indian women treated during the nineteenth century?*

Source A *A woman committing* sati, *early in the eighteenth century. The word* sati *means 'a true lady'. This picture now hangs in Bombay.*

## What was sati?

*Sati* was the custom among some Hindus of burning alive a widow in the funeral fire of her dead husband. In theory sati only happened when a woman wanted to rejoin her husband in the next life. Such a holy act was supposed to bring much respect to her family. But sometimes relatives forced a woman to commit sati because they wanted her money or because they could not afford to look after a widow.

Bentinck thought that sati was disgusting, but he was not the only reformer who wanted sati abolished. The great Hindu scholar and reformer Ram Mohan Roy (1772–1833) campaigned vigorously against sati too. In 1829, after checking with his army officers that abolition would not lead to unrest, Bentinck made sati illegal, though the practice was never completely wiped out.

## Source B

Tarabai Shinde, a Maratha woman, writes about the life of a Hindu widow.

'Once a woman's husband has died, not even a dog would want to share her position. And what is this position? The barber comes to shave all the curls and hair off her head, just to cool men's eyes. All her ornaments are taken away. Her beauty vanishes. She is exposed in all sorts of ways as if she belonged to no-one, and publicly covered in shame. She cannot even go to any wedding or reception which married women attend.'

Tarabai Shinde, *Stri-purusha-tulana*, 1882

51

Source C  *Committing* sati. *This painting shows a widow burning on the funeral fire of her husband, about a century after the woman in Source A.*

## Source E

Pandit Panchanadi Guttalal Ghanashyamaji, a Hindu scholar of Bombay, comments on the role of women in Hindu society.

'The truth, however, is that a woman is a thing to be enjoyed. The bride is given by her father to the bridegroom … The thing called woman is the greatest of all the objects of enjoyment in this world, and is not, like a house, capable of being enjoyed by the husband's relations. The woman is not fit for remarriage and enjoyment by a stranger. Like a dining leaf [used in India for eating off, like a plate] once used by another man she is unfit to be enjoyed by another man.'

Government of India Records, 1886

## Source D

Part of the 1829 *sati* regulation.

'All persons convicted of helping in the sacrifice of a Hindu widow, by burning or burying her alive, whether the sacrifice be voluntary on her part or not, shall be guilty of murder, and shall be punished by fine or by both fine and imprisonment. A plea that the act is justified on the grounds that the woman being sacrificed asked for assistance in putting her to death will not be upheld.'

Sati Regulation XVII, AD 1829 of the Bengal Code, 4 December 1829

---

**1** Study Source A. What evidence is there in this picture to support the suggestion that *either* this act of sati was voluntary *or* this woman was forced to commit sati?

**2** Look at Source C. What differences between Source A and Source C can you find? How do you explain these differences?

**3** How does Source B help to explain why some women might commit sati voluntarily?

**4** Sati was abolished in 1829. What does Source E tell us about the position of women in the late nineteenth century?

# 18

# The rebellion of 1857–58

*The British nearly lost control of India in 1857. Thousands of Indian soldiers, known as sepoys, mutinied and killed their British officers. Indian landlords and peasants rebelled against British rule and rallied to support the traditional Mughal and Maratha leaders.*

*Why did the rebellion happen?*

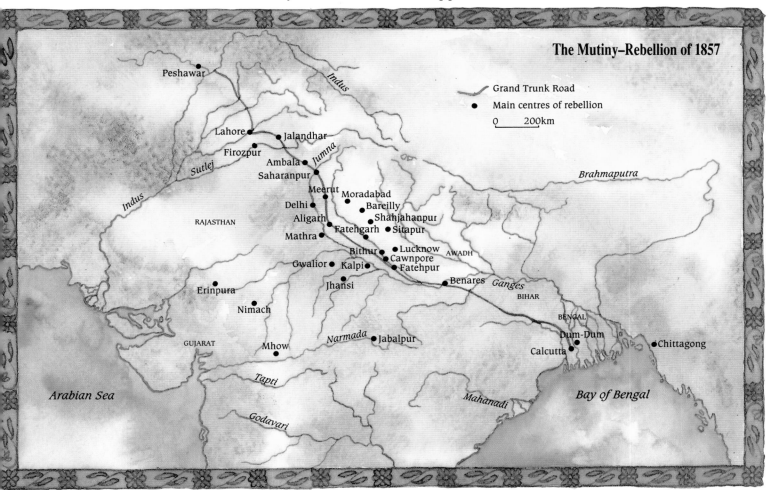

The Mutiny–Rebellion of 1857

## Explosion at Meerut

The rebellion began with the mutiny of the sepoys in Meerut on 10 May 1857. That night, the rebels marched on Delhi, which was 64 km (40 miles) away. The rebels met with little resistance, and the revolt was soon spreading like wildfire throughout much of north India.

The British were slow to react at first: they did not pursue the rebels who marched from Meerut to Delhi. Instead they decided to protect the white people living in Meerut. It was a full month before they could get together a large force to send to Delhi. It took until the middle of 1858 for the British to win back control over north India.

## Why did the Indians rebel?

There were many reasons why the sepoys mutinied and the peasants and princes rebelled. The main ones are listed in the boxes overleaf.

# The causes of the rebellion

- Sepoys who had been recruited in Awadh lost certain privileges after it became part of British India in 1856. Their pay was reduced because they could no longer claim to be serving 'abroad' (that is, outside an *independent* Awadh). High taxes imposed by the British on their families in the villages would now be even harder to pay.

- A new Government Act of 1856 meant that sepoys (soldiers) had to be ready to serve overseas at any time. For strict Hindus, crossing the *kali pani* ('black seas') was unacceptable because it was against their religious beliefs.

- A rumour was spread that cartridges for the new Enfield rifle had been greased with the fat of the unclean pig and sacred cow. Biting off the end of the cartridge would therefore be sinful for both Hindu and Muslim sepoys. This rumour helped to spark off the mutiny in Meerut.

**How it was loaded**

**A greased cartridge**

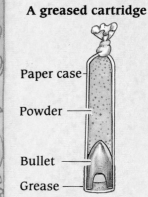

Paper case

Powder

Bullet

Grease

1   The soldier tears open the end of the cartridge with his teeth.

2   He pours the powder down the muzzle of his rifle. Then he thrusts the bullet, still wrapped in the cartridge paper which makes it a tight fit, into the muzzle.

3   He takes his ramrod from its slot beneath the rifle barrel, and rams paper, bullet and powder to the bottom of the barrel.

## Complaints in the countryside

Small landowners and peasant farmers found it difficult to pay the high taxes to the British. This was particularly hard in areas like Awadh, which had only come under British control in 1856.

The British challenged Indian customs and beliefs. For example, they abolished the Hindu custom of sati in 1829. They also wanted to introduce the Western style of education. In 1835 the use of Persian, the court language of the Mughals, was abolished in official letters, and replaced by English. Schools and colleges were set up to provide a Western education, using the English language. The work of Christian missionaries made Indians suspicious that the British were going to force everyone to become Christian.

## Grievances of the princes

Indian princes and nobles lost power and prestige when their territories were taken over by the British. They very much resented the new British rulers. The last Mughal emperor, Bahadur Shah, became the figurehead of the rebellion in Delhi. The Marathas accepted the leadership of Nana Sahib, the Peshwa, who resented the loss of his kingdom.

**The Rani of Jhansi**
*The Rani of Jhansi, India's 'Joan of Arc', who died fighting the British in June 1858. This picture was painted by an unknown artist in about 1890.*

1 Study the map on page 53. Which parts of India were most affected by the mutiny, and which parts were least affected? Where do you think the British got the troops from to put down the mutiny?

2 Study the box on 'The army reforms' on page 54. Why might some Indian sepoys be more prepared to mutiny than others?

3 Study the box on 'Grievances of the princes' on page 54. Why would the British have been worried by the support for the rebellion of people like Bahadur Shah?

4 In your own words, write down a list of reasons that each of the following might have used to justify their support for the rebellion:

◆ a peasant family
◆ an Indian sepoy
◆ an Indian prince.

The Rani was the widow of the Raja (king) of Jhansi, but with no male heirs the State of Jhansi passed to the East India Company in 1853. The Rani appealed to the British government for support, but in vain, and she grew to hate the British.

With her supporters she joined forces with the rebels and became one of their leaders. She fought with them in battles at Jhansi and Gwalior, and died fighting for the fort of Gwalior. For many years afterwards she remained a symbol of armed resistance against British rule.

# 19

# Bloodshed!

*During the rebellion of 1857–58, terrible atrocities were committed by both sides.
Many innocent Indian and British people were brutally killed.*

*Why did passions run so high?*

**Source A** *Massacre of British officers and their wives at Jhansi. From a book published in 1858.*

**Source B** *British officers and their wives trying to escape from Cawnpore. From a book also published in 1858.*

## Source C

A historian's view.

'While it is true that large numbers of European men, women and children were murdered with great brutality by the mutineers, it is equally evident that some of the stories of torture, rape and bestiality were either grossly exaggerated or totally untrue. Indeed, regarding the treatment of white women by their Pandi captors, it has not been possible to discover a single proven case of rape.

However, the British relief forces felt that every Indian male capable of carrying arms was guilty of such crimes. Hundreds were killed in the days following the recapture of Delhi, either by shooting or by slow strangulation.'

R. Perkins, *The Kashmir Gate*, 1983

## Source D  *'Justice', a cartoon from* **Punch** *magazine, September 1857.*

● *What is shown on the white woman's shield?*

---

**1** Describe what is happening to the women and children in Source A.

**2** Source B shows a massacre near Cawnpore. What are the differences between Source A and Source B?

**3** Sources A and B were published in England in 1858. In what sense does Source C cast doubt on their truthfulness?

**4** Can you suggest a motive for the artists who produced Sources A and B? Explain your answer carefully.

**5** Study Source D. Who or what is the white woman supposed to represent? Why is she so big?

**6** Explain why Source D is called 'Justice'. Does the title fit this cartoon? Explain your answer.

**7** Look again at Source D. Why do you think the cartoonist shows the British sparing the Indian women and children?

Sources D and E (see next page) are two of the so-called 'Cawnpore' cartoons. These were drawn after the massacre of women and children at Cawnpore in June and July 1857. On 27 June a large group of British refugees who had been granted a safe passage by boat away from Cawnpore were shot at: 200 were saved from the massacre, only to be killed later by butchers with knives after sepoys had refused to execute the women and children in cold blood.

**Source E** *'The British lion's vengeance on the Bengal tiger.' Another cartoon from* Punch *magazine, August 1857.*
- *Who or what does the lion represent?*
- *What is the tiger doing?*

**Source F** *Sepoys who had mutinied being blown from guns. This picture is from a book published in 1858.*

## Source G
A modern historian's view.

'Ordinary rebels often fared worse if they were caught alive, especially in the early months of the rebellion. The British tried to make them fear not only death, but misery after death.

Prisoners were blown to pieces by guns because they were thought to believe that there was no peace after death for people whose bodies were incomplete.

Others were humiliated. At Cawnpore some were forced to lick clean the bloodstained walls of the place where the women and children had been butchered, though there was no proof that they were responsible.'

F. W. Rawding, *The Rebellion in India, 1857*, published in 1977

Source H  *Some of the mutineers were hanged.*

## Source I
Thomas Cadell, who won a Victoria Cross during the siege of Delhi, wrote to his sister.

'Lots of blackguards are hanged every morning … the more the merrier … you say Delhi ought to be destroyed … we say the same.'

From the India Office Library and Records

---

**1** Look at Source F. This terrible punishment was said to have been used first by the Mughal emperors. Why do you think the British used it?

**2** Read Source G carefully. This was written 120 years after the events it describes. Does this mean that Source G must be unreliable evidence? Explain your answer.

**3** Compare Source G and Source H. Why do you think all prisoners were not dealt with in the same way? (Try to think of several possible reasons.)

**4** How do Sources A and B help to explain the attitude of the soldier in Source I? Explain your answer carefully.

**5** Why are atrocities like those shown in this unit often a feature of war and rebellion?

## The British Raj

After the rebellion of 1857–58, Queen Victoria of Britain became Empress of India, and the East India Company was abolished. The British continued to rule in India for another ninety years until 1947.

Many British people thought that the building of railways and the expansion of trade would bring prosperity to India. But poverty and famine for ordinary people remained a problem in India.

*Gandhi in London, 1931, to attend a Round Table Conference.*

## Gandhi campaigns for India's freedom

By the twentieth century, more and more Indians were demanding independence from Britain. They did not want to be a colony of the British Empire. M. K. Gandhi was the most famous campaigner for independence. He believed in using non-violent methods of protest. He led three major campaigns against British rule between 1919 and 1947.

## South Asia today

India is the largest country in modern South Asia. In 1992 its population was estimated to be 858 million. Food production has been increased to help feed the country's large population.

## Independence:
## India, Pakistan and Bangladesh

The independence movement led by Gandhi was successful. In 1947 the British handed over power to a largely Muslim Pakistan, and a largely Hindu India.

In 1971, East Pakistan became Bangladesh after fighting a war of independence against West Pakistan.

### The Nehru family.

*The Prime Minister of India in 1950, with two of the country's future Prime Ministers. The Nehru family has dominated the politics of India since 1947. Jawaharlal Nehru was the first Prime Minister of India. His daughter and grandson also became Prime Ministers, but their rule ended tragically. Nehru's daughter, Indira Gandhi, was assassinated in 1984, while her son, Rajiv Gandhi, was assassinated in May 1991.*

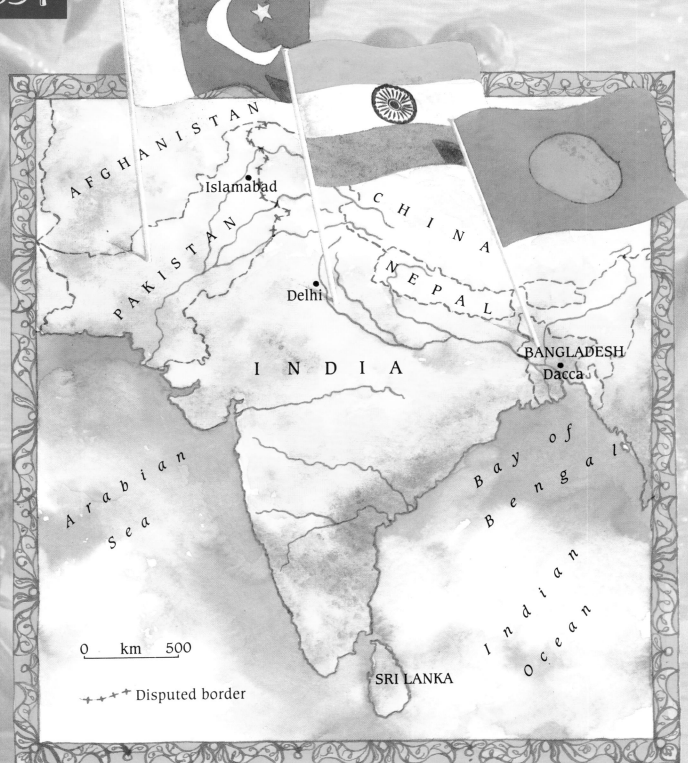

1857

# Attainment target grid

This grid is designed to indicate the varying emphases on attainment targets in the questions in each unit. It is not to be interpreted as a rigid framework, but as a simple device to help the teacher plan the study unit.

✗     some focus
✗✗    strong focus
✗✗✗   main focus

| | AT1 a | AT1 b | AT1 c | AT2 | AT3 |
|---|---|---|---|---|---|
| 1 Babur the victorious | | ✗✗✗ | | ✗ | |
| 2 Akbar: the making of a Mughal emperor | | ✗ | ✗✗✗ | | ✗ |
| 3 Akbar's empire | | ✗✗✗ | | | ✗✗ |
| 4 Village life | ✗✗ | | ✗ | | ✗ |
| 5 The roots of poverty | | ✗✗✗ | | | ✗✗ |
| 6 The lifestyle of the rich | ✗✗✗ | | | | ✗✗ |
| 7 Roads and rivers | | | ✗✗✗ | | ✗ |
| 8 A great trading empire | | ✗✗✗ | | | ✗ |
| 9 Mughal towns and cities | | | | ✗ | ✗✗✗ |
| 10 Shivaji: the challenge of the 'Mountain Rat' | | | | ✗✗ | ✗✗✗ |
| 11 Aurangzeb: your verdict? | | | | ✗✗✗ | |
| 12 The decline of the Mughals | | ✗✗✗ | | | ✗ |
| 13 The British in Bengal | | ✗✗✗ | | | ✗✗ |
| 14 The Black Hole of Calcutta | | | ✗✗ | ✗✗✗ | ✗ |
| 15 Tipu Sultan of Mysore | | ✗ | ✗✗ | ✗✗✗ | ✗ |
| 16 A meeting of two cultures | ✗✗ | | ✗✗ | | ✗✗ |
| 17 Sati: death on the flames | | | ✗✗✗ | | ✗✗ |
| 18 The rebellion of 1857–58 | | ✗ | ✗✗✗ | | ✗ |
| 19 Bloodshed! | | ✗ | ✗ | | ✗✗✗ |

# Attainment target focus

# Index